# LIFE IN VICTORIAN BRITAIN

MICHAEL ST JOHN PARKER

Dynamic, self-confident, enterprising, idealistic – Victorian Britain was a society undergoing rapid change, and readily convinced that most change was for the better. The nation's wealth was increasing, its international power and prestige were growing, and progress was the goal.

The 64-year- from 1837 to ishing progress was the age of t engineering; of manufacturing of numerous discoveries in science and medicine; and the age of Empire, when Britain ruled half the world, and Victoria herself reigned gloriously over the greatest power the world had ever seen.

The Victorian emphasis on enterprise was in harmony with the scientific discoveries of the time, as well as its economic realities. The theories of the great naturalist Charles Darwin, especially the idea of the survival of the fittest, may have shocked the Victorians, but they accorded well with the underlying instincts of a commercial and industrial nation that was deeply imbued with the individualistic values promoted by Samuel Smiles (1812–1904) in his best-selling book *Self-Help*.

# VICTORIA AND ALBERT

Queen Victoria, who was only 18 when she inherited the throne, shared the 'Victorian' social attitudes and standards of her subjects, and substantially influenced them by her own example. Through her strong Protestant faith and devotion to family values and, later, her compassionate concern for the poor and downtrodden in society, the queen gained respect for the monarchy and gave it a new place in a changing world. She '… kept her throne unshaken still, Broad-based upon the people's will.'

To begin with the young queen displayed a taste for elegant festivity that suggested Regency styles and manners. But all that changed with her marriage in 1840 to Prince Albert of Saxe-Coburg-Gotha. It was a very suitable dynastic match but it was also, beyond question, a love-match: '… It was with some emotion that I beheld Albert – who is *beautiful*!'

The Prince Consort was unpopular in England. Although he was highly accomplished, a conscientious

*ABOVE: The queen and her consort, Prince Albert, at Windsor Castle, a detail from a painting by Sir Edwin Landseer. The willingness of the royal couple to be portrayed in a style of informal domesticity contributed to the new popularity of 'family values'.*

worker, and a man of the highest integrity, he lacked ease and confidence. As a foreigner, Albert was often a source of suspicion; in the end, perhaps, the cynical English just found him too good to be true. But Victoria adored him without reservation, and adopted his style as her own, particularly after his premature death from typhoid fever in 1861.

*ABOVE RIGHT: The young queen rides out with Lord Melbourne, the minister whose shrewdly benign advice did much to shape her political awareness, and Lord John Russell, Leader of the House.*

## • FAMILY VALUES •

Victoria and Albert, seen here playing with their children in a popular print, demonstrated the essential humanity and goodness of the royal family. The 'ideal family' occupied a central position in Victorian society. This was envisaged as large, extending over three generations, and embracing unmarried daughters, maiden aunts and bachelor uncles of various ages. The family was upheld as the provider of social security, respectability, entertainment and even education in the 19th century.

*ABOVE: Sir Robert Peel and Queen Victoria. Highly principled, efficient and a great modernizer, Peel was an essentially 'Victorian' politician, yet the queen herself disliked him – 'such a cold, odd man'.*

*LEFT: The coronation of Queen Victoria in Westminster Abbey on 28 June 1838. Contemporary observers were much struck by the burst of sunlight which illuminated the moment when the crown was placed on the queen's head, symbolizing, as it seemed, a fresh dawn in the affairs of the nation.*

THE QUEEN AND PRINCE ALBERT AT HOME.

# FULL STEAM AHEAD

The foundations of Victorian prosperity were laid down during the 18th century, when scientific curiosity was married to agricultural and commercial wealth to produce technological innovations. Coal and iron, wool and cotton were the raw materials to which this technology was applied.

By the beginning of Victoria's reign the employment of steam-powered machinery had begun to transform industrial productivity, and Britain became known as the 'Workshop of the World' – leading producer of industrial goods, and chief developer of new resources and fresh markets overseas.

Coal, and the steam-power that it could generate, was the basis of Victorian industry. Between 1830 and 1870 the output of British mines rose from 17 million tons per annum to 121.3 million tons. Much of the power that was unleashed from this coal went into the manufacture of iron, and here the production figures rose from 740,000 tons in 1830 to 6,378,000 tons in 1870. Growth in the textile industries was less significant in terms of economic structures,

but still immensely impressive when measured by value: textile exports, of cotton and woollen goods, grew from £30 million in 1830 to £120 million in 1870.

The heroes of the age were the mechanical inventors, men such as James Nasmyth, who in 1842 developed a steam-hammer 'capable of cracking the top of an egg in a wine glass at one blow, and of shaking the parish at the next', and Joseph Whitworth who produced a machine capable of measuring one two-millionth of an inch. Ingenuity was richly rewarded – when Henry Bessemer started up his own firm to exploit his invention, in 1856, of a new process for manufacturing steel, he made 100 per cent profit every other month for 14 years!

*MAIN PICTURE: The Britannia railway bridge over the Menai Straits between North Wales and Anglesey, opened in 1850.*

*INSET: A triumph of engineering: a jubilant crowd celebrates the launch of the* Great Britain *at Bristol in 1843. The first all-iron steam ship, she marked the beginning of a new era in shipbuilding.*

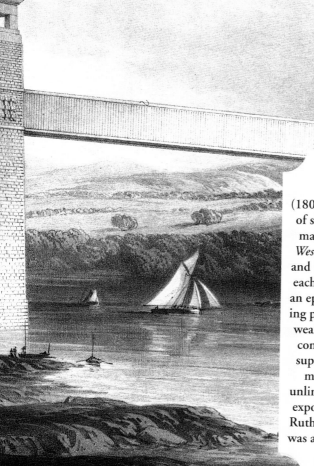

## • A MAN OF IRON •

The engineer Isambard Kingdom Brunel (1803–59) was one of the great figures in the story of shipbuilding during Victoria's reign. His three masterpieces – the *Great Western*, the *Great Britain* and the *Great Eastern*, were each of them milestones in an epic journey of engineering progress, which brought wealth to the shipbuilding communities, worldwide supremacy for the British merchant marine, and unlimited opportunities for exporters of British goods. Ruthlessly practical, Brunel was also a builder of railway bridges and tunnels.

# LIFE AT WORK

Britain's status as the 'workshop of the world' was achieved at great human cost. Men, women and young children alike were employed for excessively long hours, in conditions that were often harsh and squalid, to carry out tasks that were physically taxing and frequently dangerous. Hardship was most especially marked in the mines, where technical progress came much more slowly than in the textile factories and engineering works.

Conditions in the mining industry were extremely harsh, and the miners' sufferings continued late into the 19th century. In factories above ground, improvements were brought about by successive Factory Acts from 1819 onwards. These Acts, several of which were owed to the great philanthropist Lord Shaftesbury, progressively reduced the hours that might be worked, imposed safety regulations, and laid down certain basic requirements relating to working conditions.

**ABOVE:** *The printed 'emblem' of the shipwrights' trade union. These associations of skilled workers gave respectability and strength to the trade union movement.*

**LEFT:** *Huge numbers of women were employed in Victorian mills and factories. Here they sit in ranks, grinding pen nibs on centrally driven machinery. For Victorian society, female emancipation actually meant the freedom* not *to work.*

At the same time the labour force organized itself for its own protection, through the Trades Unions which grew in strength and status from the 1850s onwards.

In one sense, the workplace horrors of the Industrial Revolution cannot be overstated; but in another sense, they should be looked at in perspective. The vast majority of people in pre-industrial society lived in poverty, squalor, discomfort and danger. The workers who joined the new factories were fleeing an existence as agricultural labourers which was even harsher, in their eyes, than the wretchedness of life in the towns.

The demands of mechanized mass production generated by the Industrial Revolution undoubtedly did much, in the early part of the 19th century, to 'dehumanize' employers and employees alike. It was a major achievement of British society during the reign of Victoria to recover a large part of that lost dimension of humanity through social reforms and improvements in living standards.

## • A GREAT VICTORIAN •

Lord Shaftesbury inquires into the reality of slum life in London, 1840. The Victorian social reformers were motivated both by genuine compassion for the suffering poor, often born of religious conviction, and by an entirely justifiable fear of social disorder. The slums which they sought to improve were hotbeds of vice, crime and political radicalism.

*The city of Sheffield, at the heart of the Industrial Revolution, in 1879. Such scenes struck contemporaries as neither grim nor quaint – rather, they expressed the power of steam, and the capacity of the factory system to create huge wealth and raise standards of living throughout society.*

# THE CHANGING FACE OF BRITAIN

Underlying both the prosperity and the poverty of Victorian Britain was a huge increase in the population. Between the censuses of 1841 and 1901, the number of people living in the United Kingdom rose from approximately 27 million to over 41 million.

The census returns showed a steadily accelerating shift in the balance of the population between the countryside and the towns. By 1851 as much as one-third of the population lived in concentrations of 20,000 or more, and throughout the second half of the century the towns grew rapidly as a result of emigration from the countryside and the higher birth rate in the towns. London and Birmingham, Manchester and Glasgow developed during the Victorian era as centres of a new urban culture.

Despite the growth of the towns, certain features of Victorian Britain remained resolutely rural. The land-owning aristocracy lived in considerable comfort on their country estates and farms, and those who made money from industry or commerce were usually quick to invest it in land. Agriculture itself survived a difficult period in the 1840s, to enjoy 20 years of piping prosperity. This period of 'High Farming' was brought to an end, however, by imports of cheaper foreign agricultural produce in the 1870s.

The same prosperity was prompting a series of far-reaching reforms and public works in the towns and cities. The Public Health Acts of 1848 and 1875, the establishment of the Local Government Board in 1871, the Artisans' Dwellings Act of 1875, and the Local Government Acts of 1888 and

*RIGHT: Back-to-back houses in the coal port of Staithes, Yorkshire. The health risks of such overcrowding were at first not understood.*

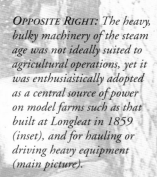

*OPPOSITE RIGHT: The heavy, bulky machinery of the steam age was not ideally suited to agricultural operations, yet it was enthusiastically adopted as a central source of power on model farms such as that built at Longleat in 1859 (inset), and for hauling or driving heavy equipment (main picture).*

*ABOVE: Much of the squalor that blighted the new towns of the 19th century was the result of haste and greedy thoughtlessness. Here a gas works is surrounded by the chaotic dwellings of the poor. However, as gas provided light, heat and power, even these slum tenements might have compared favourably with many agricultural labourers' cottages.*

## • PEEL'S PEELERS •

Systematic enforcement of the law in 19th-century Britain began with Sir Robert Peel's Metropolitan Police Act of 1829, which established a police force for London under the direct control of the Home Secretary. Manned, at first, largely by ex-army NCOs, it was speedily copied in other cities, and forces were established, also, after 1839, in rural areas. Policemen became known as 'Peelers'.

1894 were far-reaching reforms that led to substantial changes. Although slums, poverty and despair did not cease to exist, the Victorian period was one that set and achieved new standards of civilized urban life including a system of local self-government which was aptly symbolized by the majestic civic buildings that rose to dominate the skylines of numerous British towns and cities.

# HOME LIFE

Victorian Britain's unprecedented prosperity brought material comfort and security to a far greater proportion of her population than ever before. Supplies of housing and standards of house building soared; domestic equipment was transformed by the Victorian delight in mechanical ingenuity and capacity for mass-production; improvements in transport ensured a steady supply of foodstuffs and domestic goods which had previously been rare or unknown, while technical advances brought supplies of piped water, gas and, by the end of the century, electricity.

As a result of all this, the Victorian middle classes were able to enjoy standards of living that were higher, in some respects, than those of the 18th-century aristocracy. The working classes also benefited: a prudent artisan could maintain a household in real, if modest, comfort, so long as he remained in health and employment, and did not over-indulge in drink.

Servants were essential ingredients in the success of this new domesticity. All but the very poorest households needed a resident maid to help with the domestic chores, and a middle-class family might employ four or five people. At the time of the 1891 census, there were almost two million indoor servants. A servant's life might well have been described as rigorous and limited, and there were undoubtedly many cases of exploitation; but, in general terms, domestic service offered security, respectability, and valued employment and training to the vast majority of those involved.

*RIGHT: The new arrival – a baby has been born to a prosperous couple, c.1860. The two women on either side of the cradle are probably the lady's maid and the nursery maid or wet-nurse respectively. Childbirth remained dangerous and difficult throughout the 19th century, despite improvements in medical techniques.*

*ABOVE: Father carves the joint for Sunday lunch. Formal mealtimes were strictly observed by Victorian middle-class families, with a hierarchical seating plan and scrupulous table manners. The art of conversation was cultivated according to set rules.*

In this painting, The Soldier's Wife, the children play at war games, while their mother reflects unhappily on the perils facing her husband.

## • MRS BEETON •

The roles of the sexes diverged in the course of the 19th century, as women specialized in housewifery, while men worked away from the home. This was seen at the time as giving advantages to women as well as to men. Mrs Beeton, in her famous *Book of Household Management*, certainly conveyed a strong impression that the arts of housecraft were to be seen as giving power and authority to those who possessed them!

BELOW: *London hotel maids in 1892. The girl on the left is carrying a can of hot water – available on tap only in the most luxurious establishments, even at the end of Victoria's reign.*

# A VICTORIAN CHILDHOOD

The Victorian era saw a remarkable change in the treatment of children, and in society's understanding of childhood. From being seen merely as small adults, children came, instead, to be regarded as innocent, vulnerable and deserving of society's protection.

Queen Victoria herself was unsentimental in her view of small children; but she and Albert set a fashion which was widely followed, by devoting much time to caring lovingly for their children, supplying them with toys and books specially produced for their pleasure and education, and generally planning their upbringing in a far-sighted manner.

From 1842 these attitudes brought about legislation to regulate and then outlaw child labour in factories and mines and up chimney-stacks, and also for the development of schools, and for orphanages for the homeless waifs who were left without families to support them. The pre-occupation with children and childhood reflected the realities of demography. Life expectation was rising in Victorian Britain, but the population was dominated by the youthful, rather than the elderly, age groups. Thirty-five per cent of the inhabitants of Great Britain were aged under 15 in 1851. This dropped to 32 per cent in 1901 and 22 per cent in 1951, and it is estimated that it will be 12 per cent in 2001.

Interestingly, a growing preoccupation with childhood in the context of the family was not matched by developments in formal education. Limited importance was attached to schooling in Victorian times.

*ABOVE: A Victorian china doll. In fact only the head and hands, and possibly the feet, would have been made of china. Such toys would always have been highly prized, and today they have become collectors' pieces.*

*LEFT: A sentimental picture of 1891, entitled* The Pinch of Poverty, *disguises the stark reality of life for many deprived Victorian children.*

*RIGHT: Children dancing to a street organ, c.1890. Such scenes were common in an age when the street was a playground where the young could entertain themselves without fear of road traffic.*

# TOM BROWN'S SCHOOLDAYS

Thomas Hughes' morality tale about the childhood and youth of a middle-class boy in mid-Victorian England achieved enormous and lasting influence on its publication in 1857. The children's storybook also provides a fascinating, if often unreliable, view of the great headmaster Thomas Arnold, and the effect that he had on Rugby School.

TOP: *Playing football – probably less popular than bird-nesting or ratting, so far as these village boys were concerned.*

ABOVE: *Children in a toy shop, colour lithograph 1899. The late Victorian age saw a great growth in the manufacture of charming and imaginative toys, games and storybooks.*

# TIME OFF

Increasing numbers of Victorians found opportunities that their predecessors could not have had to seek recreation and enjoy themselves, often in imaginative ways.

The old country sports were still the most popular – with men, at any rate. Many countryfolk hunted the fox or followed the hunt. Horse-racing, shooting and fishing were also favoured pastimes. As the population became more urbanized, however, ball games grew in appeal. Cricket and football, golf and hockey, tennis and fives, which had existed in rudimentary forms, were enthusiastically adopted and refined by the Victorian middle classes.

Some sports that had been popular until the early 19th century – bull-running, bear-baiting and cock-fighting – were outlawed, and boxing was converted from a contest to destruction into a demonstration of skill and strength. Professionalism began to compete with the amateur ideal in sport.

The less strenuous pleasures of town life also flourished. Nineteenth-century English theatre was characterized by melodrama, but there was much music-making, especially choral singing, and the works of novelists and poets were eagerly devoured, and often read aloud. Parlour games were popular but cards were frowned upon as too much like gambling.

## • PHOTOGRAPHY •

Street photography (above) became a popular pastime in the public parks by the 1870s. W.H. Fox Talbot, a descendant of the Earls of Shrewsbury, was the pioneer of photography in Britain. In 1838 he succeeded in making photographic prints on silver chloride paper, and his *Pencil of Nature* was the first photographically illustrated book. Fine examples of his work can be seen at his home, Lacock Abbey in Wiltshire, now a National Trust property.

**BELOW:** *Cremorne Gardens, 1864. Recreation gardens popular in 18th-century London, such as Vauxhall and Ranelagh, continued to be enjoyed by the Victorians. Increasingly, however, their rather racy, sometimes seedy, reputations brought them disapproval.*

**ABOVE:** *Music halls, where men and women could meet and drink to the accompaniment of music or other entertainment, flourished particularly at the end of the Victorian era.*

**ABOVE:** *A Vanity Fair cartoon of W.G. Grace, the great cricketer, in 1877. He played a unique part in elevating cricket to its status as the national game.*

**MAIN PICTURE:** *Paddling at the seaside. Previously seen as a source of medicinal treatment, the seaside became hugely popular with everyone in Victorian society, headed by the queen herself.*

# THE RAILWAY AGE

The foundations of what is often called the 'Transport Revolution' had been laid in Britain in the 18th century, with the development of the canal system and the introduction of turnpike roads. The reign of Queen Victoria, however, saw astonishing developments in transport both by land and by sea, as well as the tentative beginnings of air transport.

The railway engine – built of iron, fuelled by coal, powered by steam – revolutionized the industrial economy, transformed the lives of the population, and irrevocably linked the town and countryside. The first public railway, between Stockton and Darlington, was opened in 1825; by 1850, some 7,000 miles of line had been built, and by the end of the century that mileage had been tripled again. Great fortunes were made in the process by contractors such as George Hudson and Thomas Brassey; rather less came the way of the engineers, such as the Stephensons, father and son, and Isambard Kingdom Brunel who built the Great Western Railway.

*ABOVE: A horse tram in London, about 1870. These extraordinary vehicles could carry up to 46 passengers, though not at any great speed. This service ran along the riverside levels between Pimlico, Peckham, Camberwell and Greenwich.*

*St Pancras Station, seen from the east along the Pentonville Road, in 1884. The station is one of the great achievements of Victorian Gothic architecture.*

# • THE POSTAL SERVICE •

The development of a regular and efficient postal service by Sir Rowland Hill during the 1840s brought about great changes in both economic and social life, as communications became easier, faster and cheaper. The Penny Black stamp of 1840 (right) was the first postage stamp in the world. The Victorians were enthusiastic letter writers, who made full use of a service of several collections and deliveries every day.

*LEFT: An early telegraph machine, 1837.*

*ABOVE: Queen Victoria survived a number of more or less serious attempts on her life. One of the most dramatic, in 1872, saw her faithful Highland servant, John Brown, spring to the rescue.*

*LEFT: A London Underground train passing through Portland Street Station on a trial run in 1862. The early Underground trains were drawn by steam engines, and travel on them must have been dirty and uncomfortable.*

# THE GREAT EXHIBITION

The enormous Crystal Palace Exhibition of 1851 was intended as a demonstration of Britain's economic supremacy, and as a celebration, through science, trade and industry, of the triumph of peace and progress. Prince Albert took a leading part in the planning and organization of the exhibition, which was, in the end, a personal triumph for him.

The marvellous structure which housed the exhibits, and gave its name to the whole event, was built by Joseph Paxton (1801–65). His concept of a structure in iron and glass showed him to be an inventive genius of engineering:

*As though 'twere by a wizard's rod*
*A blazing arch of lucid glass*
*Leaps like a fountain from the grass*
*To meet the sun.*

The contents of the Exhibition were immensely varied, and ranged from the most practical – examples of the latest manufacturing machinery – to the highly pretentious – 'pleasing objects' that were heavily adorned but totally useless. Ingenuity of design and manufacture and the application of steam power were particularly prized.

The Great Exhibition attracted vast crowds and the profits of the event paid for the establishment of the Science Museum, the Natural History Museum, and the Victoria and Albert Museum.

*TOP, CENTRE AND BELOW RIGHT:*
*Much of the Great Exhibition was devoted to a celebration of British imperial achievement and the Indian section was a centre of attention. The stuffed elephant was procured, with some difficulty, from a museum in Saffron Walden.*

## • MARITIME TRADE •

Overseas trade, the lifeblood of the British economy, increased rapidly during Victoria's reign. Imports rose from an annual average of approximately £40,000,000 in 1830 to approximately £570,000,000 by 1900, and exports from approximately £46,500,000 to approximately £330,000,000. Steam ships competed with increasing effectiveness as carriers of this trade from the 1840s onwards, and even the fastest clippers, such as the *Cutty Sark* (above), seen here overhauling the mail steamer *Britannia*, eventually became redundant.

*BELOW: The construction of the Crystal Palace, the first building of any size to be entirely prefabricated, was acclaimed as one of the engineering marvels of its age. Joseph Paxton showed innovative genius in developing a style of architecture entirely befitting the new materials he was using.*

# ART AND SOCIETY

To 20th-century eyes much, though not all, of Victorian art and architecture appears over-rich, elaborately decorative and lacking in originality. The Victorian spirit expressed itself with freedom and force, however, in novels and literary forms such as poetry. Among the novelists, Charles Dickens (1812–70) was pre-eminent, and among the poets, Alfred, Lord Tennyson (1809–92). Both were the idols of society in their times.

Dickens' writings spanned a broad range of themes, and varied in style from the richly comic to the heart-rendingly tragic. He depicted Victorian society in all its variety, its richness and its

*RIGHT AND BELOW: Destitute children, whose sufferings were memorably publicized by Dickens in such works as* Oliver Twist, *could usually hope for no better fate than to be accommodated in the workhouses created by the Poor Laws. However, from 1867 onwards, Dr Thomas Barnardo (1845–1905) led the way in founding proper children's homes.*

*OPPOSITE LEFT: The Ragged School movement was set up to educate the vast numbers of slum children. Although better than nothing at all, the schools were roundly condemned for their inhumanity by Charles Dickens (above).*

**The strain of whimsical fantasy in the English literary tradition is represented with exquisite grace and charm by the writings of Lewis Carroll (C.L. Dodgson), a bachelor and mathematical don at Christ Church, Oxford. The stories with which he entertained Alice Liddell, the daughter of a colleague, were turned, in *Alice's Adventures in Wonderland* (1865) and *Through the Looking-Glass* (1871), into classics of children's literature.**

squalor; the family, childhood and poverty were the subjects to which he returned time and again, and everything he wrote was vibrant with passionate feeling.

Dickens was a campaigning novelist and his books define all the great Victorian social controversies: the faults of the legal system, dangers to public health, the horrors of factory employment, scandals in private schools, corruption in government, the miseries of prostitution. Dickens' moral intensity was matched only by his creative imagination and by the enthusiasm of his public's response.

Tennyson, who became Poet Laureate in 1850, was similarly idolized by the Victorians, but more for his mastery of descriptive and evocative language than for any campaigning tendencies. His greatest poems, *In Memoriam* and *The Idylls of the King,* are supreme expressions of Victorian Romanticism. His poem *The Charge of the Light Brigade* celebrated a high point of patriotic fervour during the Crimean War. He was outspoken in his admiration of Prince Albert and, perhaps in return, the queen was devoted to his poetry.

*LEFT: A detail from* The Lady of Shallot, *a painting by J. W. Waterhouse of Tennyson's sweetly tragic poem on the ill-fated love of Elaine, the fair maid of Astolat, and Sir Launcelot. This marked the high tide of Victorian literary Romanticism, inspired the Pre-Raphaelite school of painters, and gave fresh impetus to the Arthurian legend.*

# POLITICS AND RELIGION

Two ideas above all dominated the minds of men and women of Victorian Britain: they were reform and religion, the twin passions of the 19th century. Often, in fact, these themes were inseparable. It was moral fervour born of religious conviction that inspired reforming statesmen such as Lord Shaftesbury and John Bright, while, equally, the vigour with which religious controversies were carried on owed much to the assumption that Church matters carried political significance.

The Parliamentary Reform Acts of 1832, 1867 and 1884, supported by lesser Acts such as the Municipal Reform Act of 1882, altered the constitution by cumulative stages, rather than by sudden transformation. If the process of change was gradual, however, it was nonetheless far-reaching. By 1901 the untidy, aristocratic federation that had been 18th-century Britain had been reshaped as a highly organized unitary state, strongly administered by an elected government in London which was closely scrutinized by what the

*ABOVE: The Crimean War stirred strong emotions in Victorian Britain, sparked by instant reporting from the war front by means of the telegraph machine. The queen led public feeling with her pride in the bravery of her army, and her intense concern and sympathy for the suffering endured by the soldiers.*

*ABOVE: An infant baptism ceremony. Religious belief and family values went hand in hand throughout the 19th century, regardless of political developments and the sensational theories of Charles Darwin.*

*Illustrated London News* loved to call the 'Imperial Parliament'.

The monarchy had been peacefully relegated to a dignified, presiding role; the aristocracy had seen their influence diminished; the wealthy middle classes had taken control of the political system; and the working classes had begun their own ascent to organized power. Political ideas were pursued with articulate enthusiasm by all levels of society, whose aspirations were strikingly expressed in the great buildings of Westminster and Whitehall.

If Victorian political history was characterized by optimistic advance, the story of religion in the same period, while no less lively and controversial, was marked by long-term decline.

## • CHARLES DARWIN •

Charles Darwin's voyage to the South Seas in HMS *Beagle*, during the years 1831–36, laid the foundation for a lifetime devoted to zoological and geological analysis, conducted entirely in an inquiring, rather than a campaigning spirit. His *Origin of Species by Means of Natural Selection*, published in 1859, caused impassioned debate, and shook the foundations of religious belief for many people.

Evangelical influences remained powerful, and the Oxford Movement led by John Keble and John Henry Newman liberated a surge of spirituality which re-invigorated both the Anglican and the Roman Catholic Churches. But more and more people, as the century wore on, came to see religion as meaning little more than respectability.

Religion, however, continued to be the inspiration of writers, architects, painters and, above all, social reformers throughout the reign of Queen Victoria.

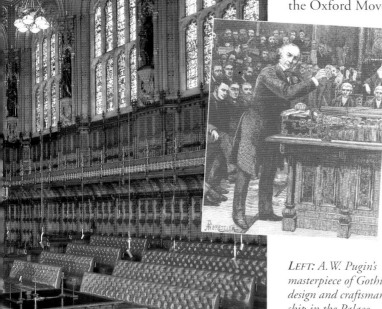

*LEFT: A.W. Pugin's masterpiece of Gothic design and craftsmanship in the Palace of Westminster, as rebuilt 1840–52. He produced 2,000 drawings for this room alone.*

*ABOVE: Prime Minister Gladstone explains his scheme for Irish Home Rule to the House of Commons, April 1886. The Irish Question, itself in origin a religious matter, came to dominate Victorian politics, and radically affected the development of the constitution.*

# INVENTIONS AND DISCOVERIES

Discovery, invention and the solving of problems clearly appealed especially to the Victorian temperament. Profit was not necessarily a primary incentive; some of the most significant discoveries were made in pursuit of scientific knowledge, and others out of an idealistic desire to benefit humanity and reduce suffering.

An example of the pure scientist was Michael Faraday, who devoted his life to the discovery and understanding of electricity. Faraday was the son of a blacksmith, and largely self-taught. Like many other talented men, he was given encouragement and practical support by Prince Albert. The applications of Faraday's discoveries, ranging from electric telegraphy in 1837 to wireless telegraphy in 1901, allow him a claim to be regarded as the father of modern technology.

The sufferings of the sick and injured presented a special challenge, which was taken up by numerous men and women. The agonies of operations undergone without anaesthetic were progressively eased from the 1840s onwards by the use of gases such as ether, first applied in 1846 by an American dentist, W.T. Morton, and chloroform, which rapidly became fashionable after Queen Victoria, in characteristically pioneering style, used it in childbirth in 1853.

Practical devices such as stethoscopes improved physicians' understanding of their patients' condition, and radical advances in surgery became possible after the realisation in the 1850s of the connection between dirt and infection. Joseph Lister introduced antiseptic techniques from 1860 onwards. The great hospital buildings of the period stand as lasting memorials to his genius.

*ABOVE: Elizabeth Garrett Anderson (1836–1917), who fought for the right of women to practise medicine. Despite intense male opposition, she was appointed visiting physician to the East London Hospital in 1870.*

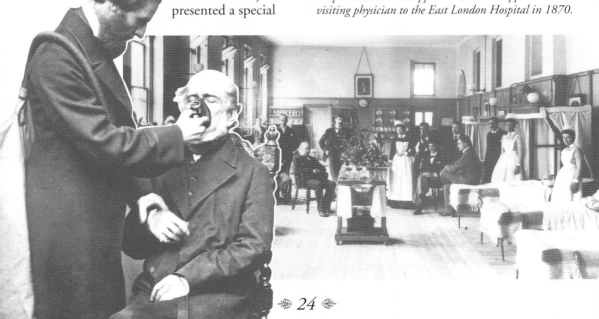

*LEFT AND INSET:*
*Michael Faraday*
*(1791–1867),*
*the English physicist who*
*discovered the principles*
*of the electric motor and*
*dynamo. Faraday's*
*experiments led to such*
*inventions as the telegraph,*
*the telephone and the*
*electric light.*

*BELOW LEFT: In early Victorian times city dwellers regularly fell victim to outbreaks of disease resulting from poor public hygiene. The river Thames was a particular source of infection. This cartoon appeared in* Punch *in 1858, at the time of a virulent cholera epidemic.*

# THE LADY
## • WITH THE LAMP •

*OPPOSITE FAR LEFT: First steps in the science of anaesthesia: J.G. Clover (1825–1882) administers chloroform to a patient. Used in the first instance to ease the pains of childbirth, and in dentistry, chloroform and its successors rapidly became essential to the practice of surgery.*

*OPPOSITE LEFT: Joseph Lister (1827–1912), pioneer of the principles of antiseptic surgery, seen with his staff at King's College Hospital, London in 1893. Lister's innovations transformed hospital practices from 1860 onwards, and saved countless lives.*

Florence Nightingale (1820–1910), 'the Lady with the Lamp', showed great courage and ruthless determination in pressing for the reform of medical services in the British army, and the organization and general development of the nursing profession. Her finest hour came when she volunteered to lead the nursing team at Scutari Base Hospital during the Crimean War.

# THE BRITISH EMPIRE

Queen Victoria's reign opened with wars in Canada, Afghanistan, and China, and hardly a year passed without some outbreak of fighting. The British were by no means always successful; in fact, there were many defeats, as at Kabul in 1842, Majuba in 1881, or Khartoum in 1885, and some major disasters, above all the terrible Indian Mutiny of 1857–58.

Not everyone, in the earlier part of the reign at least, approved of the growth of Britain's overseas empire, but few found anything wrong in the whirlwind dynamism which seemed to be driving the nation in the middle years of the 19th century, and it was that

*ABOVE: A British military encampment during the period of the Indian Mutiny.*

*LEFT: Queen Victoria in 1890, wearing her small diamond crown, the ribbon and star of the Garter and the badges of the Orders of Victoria and Albert, and of the Crown and India.*

## • AFRICAN EXPLORATION •

The 'Dark Continent', as Africa was commonly known in the Victorian era, was explored and mapped by intrepid European travellers, including the missionary David Livingstone. At the age of 24 he was inspired to leave his work in a Scottish cotton mill to become a missionary doctor, and from then until his death in 1873 he travelled over vast tracts of Central Africa. Among his discoveries was the Victoria Falls on the river Zambezi. Livingstone campaigned tirelessly against the African slave trade.

dynamism which, in due course, pushed the frontiers outwards to create the greatest empire the world had ever seen.

The whole of the Indian sub-continent was effectively in British hands by 1860, and eastward expansion continued. In 1875 the Conservative Prime Minister Benjamin Disraeli purchased a major interest in the Suez Canal, linking Britain's strategic interests in west and east. Similarly, he invested the idea of empire with a new glamour when he had Queen Victoria proclaimed Empress of India in 1876, to her great delight.

The great unknown continent of Africa, opened up by explorers from the 1860s onwards, became the setting for imperial rivalries from the 1870s, and eventually, at the very end of Victoria's reign, the scene for a struggle, the Second Boer War (1899–1902), which signalled the decline of the empire.

The Victorian Empire began with the need to safeguard trade, and to acquire resources for trading. But later, it came to overtax a home economy which was already beginning to suffer from international competition.

*The ceremonial festivals of Empire were important diplomatic occasions as well as opportunities for display and magnificence. Here native Indian princes are seen arriving in camp for the Durbar or imperial assemblage, in Delhi in 1877.*

# MODERN TIMES

What we think of as the modern world had its beginnings in the 19th century and, of those beginnings, a great deal can be credited directly to the Victorians. Theirs is a record of Herculean endeavour, brilliant originality, epic struggle and masterly co-operation, all concentrated into a period of no more than three generations.

The consequences of their efforts have spread outwards to affect every member of the human race, and the energy that they released has had a galvanic effect on every part of the globe. Centuries of social, economic, religious and political evolution led up to this moment – for it was no more than a moment, in the long perspective of history – of convulsive, almost cataclysmic effort. Indeed, it is possible to see the dynamism of Victorian England as pivotal to world history, and an episode of unique creativity.

But this was not just a period, it was a reign. It was Queen Victoria's personality

*LEFT: The celebrations of Queen Victoria's Diamond Jubilee in 1897 were intended as tributes to a great monarch and a reign of unprecedented achievement. Britain was the world's greatest power, and her prospects seemed unlimited. The pomp and ceremony marked the zenith of empire.*

*LEFT AND BELOW: An Ericsson table telephone of 1890, and an early telephone exchange. Instant communications were becoming a way of life before the end of Victoria's reign.*

*BELOW LEFT: The first underground railway, the Metropolitan Line, opened in 1863, and by the end of the Victorian era London's underground system was approximately in its modern form.*